THE ABDUCTION PREVENTION LIBRARY™

TEN STEPS TO STAYING SAFE

Cynthia MacGregor

The Rosen Publishing Group's
PowerKids Press™
New York

Published in 1999 by The Rosen Publishing Group, Inc.
29 East 21st Street, New York, NY 10010

First Edition

Book Design: Danielle Primiceri

Photo Illustrations: Cover © Seth Dinnerman; pp. 4, 7, 8, 11, 12, 15, 16, 19, 20 © Donna M. Scholl.

MacGregor, Cynthia.
    Ten steps to staying safe/ by Cynthia MacGregor.
       p.   cm. — (The abduction prevention library)
    Includes index.
    Summary: Provides tips for staying safe while dealing with strangers, including walking with a buddy, knowing your name and phone number, and knowing what to do when home alone.
    ISBN 0-8239-5248-7
    1. Safety education—Juvenile literature. 2. Children and strangers—Juvenile literature. 3. Child abuse—Prevention—Juvenile literature. [1. Strangers. 2. Safety.] I. Title.
    II. Series.
HQ770.7.M297 1998
613.6'083—dc21
                                                  97-573215
                                                   CIP
                                                       AC

Contents

Step 1 - Dial 911 for Help

Most of the people around us are nice. But some people are not so nice. And some people might even want to hurt you. The good news is that you can learn some things to do to keep yourself safe. This book tells you about ten of those things.

The first step is very easy. And it works anywhere: Call 911 if you're in trouble. You can call from home, from someone else's house, or outside at a pay phone. 911 is a free phone call.

◄ *911 is a phone number that you can rely on if you're in trouble.*

Step 2 - Keep Calm

The second step to staying safe is to keep calm. If you find yourself in a **situation** (sit-choo-AY-shun) that feels strange or makes you **uncomfortable** (un-KUMF-ter-buhl), don't **panic** (PA-nik). Instead, keep calm and think first. What's the safest thing for you to do? Is there a police officer nearby? Or is there a store where you can go for help? By keeping calm, you are helping yourself figure out the safest, smartest thing to do.

Staying calm in a scary situation can help save you from harm. ▶

Step 3 - Don't Talk to Strangers

A stranger is someone you don't know. We can't tell which strangers are nice just by looking at them. And you shouldn't trust someone just because he looks nice or has a friendly smile. So how do know who you can talk to? You don't. The smartest thing to do is don't talk to any strangers. Your safety is more important. Don't worry about being rude by not talking to a stranger who talks to you. A good person will understand why you won't talk.

◄ *Get away from a stranger who keeps trying to talk to you.*

Step 4 - Don't Be Fooled

What if a stranger drove up beside you when you were walking to your friend's house? You would do the smart thing and **ignore** (ig-NOR) her. But what if she offered you some candy or an ice-cream cone to get into the car with her? What if she said her kitten was missing and asked you to help her find it? What would you say?

No matter what a stranger offers you, say no and walk away quickly. Don't be fooled by any of these tricks.

Never accept anything from a stranger, ▶
no matter how tempting it is.

Step 5 - Walk with a Buddy

The fifth step to staying safe is to always walk with a buddy. If you walk to and from school every day, do the safe thing. Walk with a friend. If there's one day when one of you has to walk alone, make another plan. Ask your mom or dad to drive you to school and pick you up afterward. Or you and your parent could even walk home together.

Walking with a buddy is not only the safe thing to do, but it's also more fun than walking alone.

Step 6 - Know Your Names and Numbers

Step number one says that you can call 911. But you should also know your own home phone number. And what about your parents? If you can, find out their phone numbers at work. Know both their first and last names. Does your parent have a different last name than you do? You should know that too. You can **memorize** (MEH-mor-yz) these names and numbers. Or you can write them on a card and carry it with you.

Another important name or word to know is a secret code word. Only you, your parents, and a person you can trust will know what it is. That way, you know you can trust the person who knows your code word. ▶

Step 7 - Carry Emergency Money

You should always carry **emergency** (ee-MER-jen-see) money. You might need money to call your mom on a pay phone to pick you up after school. Or what if you miss the bus? If it's okay with your parents to take the public bus in an emergency, you will need some money to pay for the trip. What if you forgot your lunch one day? You can't skip lunch, so you will need money to buy a sandwich. Keep the money in a safe place. Good places include a pocket in your backpack or an inside pocket of your jacket.

◀ *Remember: You should only use your emergency money for emergencies!*

Step 8 - Know Your Home - Alone Tips

If you ever have to stay home alone, you and your parent can make a list of things you should do to stay safe. Does your mom want you to open the door for a neighbor? Should you answer the phone? You and your parent can talk about these things. Find out the answers to these questions. You can write them down and put the list where you will see it.

You can ask your parent to explain each tip to you as you write them down. Then your tip list will make more sense to you. ▶

Step 9 - Sometimes No Is Okay

Joey was waiting for his mom after basketball practice. A man came up to him.

"Can you help me find the park?" he asked. "I'm supposed to meet my son there."

"It's over there," Joey said, pointing.

"Can't you show me?" the man asked.

"No," Joey said. Then he ran into the gym.

Joey's mom had taught him about being polite. But Joey also knew that he shouldn't talk to strangers. Joey knew that it's okay to say no to something that makes you uncomfortable.

Doing what you need to in order to feel safe is much more important than talking to a stranger.

Step 10 - Stay Smart

The tenth step to staying safe is to be smart. You've learned some important tips for staying safe wherever you are. But most important, keep calm and listen to your **instincts** (IN-stinkts). If something feels scary or wrong, then it probably is. You can trust your instincts about certain situations. Remember: Your safety comes first!

Glossary

emergency (ee-MER-jen-see) A sudden need for quick action.

ignore (ig-NOR) To not pay attention to something.

instincts (IN-stinkts) The feelings that each of us has inside of us that gives us hints about what to do in certain situations.

memorize (MEH-mor-yz) To learn something and be able to repeat it.

panic (PA-nik) An uncontrolled feeling of fear.

situation (sit-choo-AY-shun) A problem; an event that happens.

uncomfortable (un-KUMF-ter-buhl) Feeling scared and unsure of yourself.

Index